urban jungle mystic

A Collection of Poems
----2009-2015----

Daniel DeLafe

Phoenix Pyre Publishing
2015

First published in the United States by Phoenix Pyre Publishing

First Edition: Revised June, 2018

Front and back cover photographs by the author.
Cover design by the author.
Photographs in text taken by the author.
Illustration at the end by the author.
Photograph of the author taken by Tamara Fernandez in Salem, MA.

ISBN: 1508943141
ISBN-13: 978-1508943143

To my grandmother, Gloria,
my Matriarch,
my foundation stone.

CONTENTS

"Life is not a series of gig lamps symmetrically arranged; life is a luminous halo, a semitransparent envelope surrounding us from the beginning of consciousness to the end."

— Virginia Woolf

"Words are timeless. You should utter them or write them with a knowledge of their timelessness."
— Kahlil Gibran

ACKNOWLEDGMENTS

I would like to acknowledge all of the family, friends, acquaintances, strangers, and experiences that have shaped me through this conversation of life. Although alone in our individual stories, it is our dynamics *together* that shape those stories, even if traveled solitarily. I would name you all one by one, but I would have to print another book just for that.

urban jungle mystic

INTRODUCTION

The writings in this volume were conceived and composed between the summer of 2009 through the first quarter of 2015, from just before turning nineteen-years-old to twenty-four, spanning from right before college to half a year after graduating Kean University in Union County, New Jersey, where I received a Bachelor's Degree in English & Writing. I have many other pieces I wasn't too satisfied with (a lot of which was honestly just messing around) but I consider these the 'cream of my crop'—if I may be permitted this cliché by the scripturiant gods—from the past few years. Although I must confess, I am still not too confident in them despite receiving a degree in writing, probably because this is my first book published.

Some pieces are quite close to how they came out at the time I wrote them, with little revision, while others were transformed over time, dramatically in some cases. Some were newly written for this volume. I choose these years because they represent a pivotal chapter in my life as a writer 'finding himself,' all former attempts still child's play. In a sense, these poems reflect a sort of 'coming of age' tale, and I hope you will witness a gradual maturity through each piece.

To be frank, over the years I began to focus on academic-type writing and scholarly reading more than creative writing and literature, and have been working on a bigger book on research into various oddities. Yet writing in general, especially poetry, has always been a personal venting process for me, even if I sometimes put it on display publicly for succorance. Like most writers, I usually wrote poetry in the midst of emotional and mental turmoil, which is why many of the poems are rather contemplative or brooding. Whether I refined them and chose to share them on the internet in my earlier years for feedback (a lot of which I subsequently came to not like), or just outright hated them and scrapped them immediately, or simply chose not to share them at all, they are, nonetheless, *little word paintings* of my inner states of mind and emotions. They served their purpose: to pour that image out in order to vicariously look at what I was thinking and feeling, and to better analyze how and why—if not soon after they have been written, then later.

My narratives and verses are Rorschach tests administered to myself; they are a deck of Tarot cards laying out past and present conditions, and future possibilities, in personal as well as impersonal transcendent archetypes. In fact, it was the writings I found most embarrassing that were often the most insightful, and led to self-transformation over the years, even if not at the time they were written; whether it was insight into the amateur mechanics of how it was written or insight regarding the distressed, often irrational state of mind I was undergoing when I wrote it (which makes me laugh at myself when I read my earlier work). Attempting to string words together in abstract or pictorial ways is therapy for me, just like music and visual art; yet as much as it is a release, it is also a labor—it is a vulnerable and painful outpouring of thought and emotion. Doubtlessly, I'm certain any creative people reading this can understand these sentiments.

Aside from the more obvious esoteric, philosophical, and political themes, as well images from my own historical atmosphere, some of these pieces intertwine those themes into dealing with my sexuality and relationships. The earlier pieces incorporating this theme veiled my struggle in spiritual symbols, such as myself as a moon and the object of desire as the sun that could liberate me. Typical, I know! They deal with falling in love for the first time (an underdeveloped, hopelessly romantic idea of love) before neither I nor my future-lover 'came out' as homosexual to each other or to anyone else. Then the 'coming out process'—the fear of rejection, uncertainty of whether or not to tell him and risk scaring him away, telling family and friends, thinking about how others would look at me, and all that jazz—these were the driving forces in some of my earliest attempts at writing poetry. I hid this struggle in symbols.

Those early poems were cries for attention. In retrospect I now see the irrational naiveté of an 18-19-year-old relying on needing another person to feel whole and complete, which was a necessary lesson to learn. Yet the whole experience also had to happen in order for me to 'come out' and become happier with myself *without* needing another person. And, of course, to conquer the fear of being defined by my sexual proclivities by a world that is just barely beginning to accept me as I am[1]—to not have that aspect of myself, as a human being, mark me as some kind of outsider when it is out of my control, or even to just have it color over whatever else I did. Ironically, I'm allowing that to happen by even writing this, and that is because it inevitably *does* color who I am. It is a part of me that cannot be altered. It influenced some of my choices in specific ways.

Although infantile and sometimes scaturient to my own eyes, I share these often depressing earlier poems because they are representations of an important part of my life, stones laid on a path toward the current man writing this sentence. Yet stones do not encompass the path of life, for it is not linear but cyclical and all-encompassing. Consciousness "is not a series of gig lamps" as Virginia Woolf wrote—it is a "luminous halo" surrounding us from birth to death, our thoughts always swirling in a pool of past, present, and possibilities of the future. Who we are becoming is

---

[1] I should note here that although I am very critical of my own country, I am not blind to the privileges (key word) I have for living in this part (key phrase) of the United States, especially as a homosexual, nor am I ungrateful for it.

3

always a seed inside of us. How much we consciously *participate in that becoming* is a matter of *labor*. I know and live the reality that writing is a profound act of participating and unraveling our luminous halo of consciousness. Such an unraveling is why some poems were more reworked over time than others, many being better understood by, or becoming clearer, to the author much later than their initial conception. In this luminous halo, the young man in those early poems was frightened, and withdrew inside himself, which is why many of those earlier pieces lack specific imagery (any found in them now were added later). They are self-centered dialogues using vague symbols—me before and during my first semester of college: hopeless, confused, and in the closet. Yet the double meaning behind the symbolism likens this longing for a lover to the longing for knowledge and wisdom.

There are those pieces conceived of in the midst of my aforementioned relationship and in the middle of my undergraduate years—more mature, but still full of mostly angst about the world, unable to define the line between what can possibly be changed within ourselves and in our society, and what may just be inevitable parts of existence, perhaps a deeper Cosmic Law nearly beyond our understanding.[2] A world full of vehemence, violence, radical belief frenzies, conspiring, poverty, debt, war crimes, splitting atoms, covert experimentation, and weird objects flying around in the skies, being covered up by various powerful institutions and psychopathic leaders, and all of the suffering. Sprinkled with some joy and friendship, of course! I wasn't completely unhappy, especially after beginning the process of 'coming out' and being with someone I was in love with.

Looking back, in many ways I was still selfish, cynical, and gullible, yet maintained a burning desire to understand the nature of evil, and why the world is the way it is, which remains at my core. We will not know what is beyond our understanding until we

---

[2] Still working on that, honestly.

4

keep trying to understand as much as we can. I would rather know uncomfortable harsh truths about my world and my surroundings than put my head in the dirt for the sake of comfort, which I came to understand was far more dangerous than enduring the depression that can accompany knowledge. That became my drive during college, yet it was a drive for *life itself as a school*.

I began to dabble in protests in Manhattan, both as a participant and vicarious observer of class war, political, religious and racial frustrations. Over the years: from Occupy Wall Street in New York, as well as one visit to the Washington D.C. encampment, to a couple of anti-nuclear/anti-war demonstrations, demonstrations on my university campus against the administration and the university president when he was exposed as a fraud by the Kean Federation of Teachers, the March Against Monsanto, up to a recent protest I attended after I graduated, during Israel's Operation "Protective" Edge in the summer of 2014, across from the United Nations headquarters. I saw a great amount of diversity at these events, and although often ambivalent about some of the views and opinions of many I encountered on these occasions, I went anyway because I felt strongly about the issues at hand—well, about the whole damn 'system,' really—and I wanted to better understand what was happening in my vicinity, among other discontent people, to write about it in the future. This book seemed as good a time as any to start.

Then there are those poems written after graduation and during a big break-up, when I finally 'explored others' while lost and confused again, a brief 'make-up,' and finally moving on from my first love. Ending with those in which I begin to find myself, in a sense, but continue to struggle with love, loss, and loneliness, and even a new muse I could not hold onto and should not have tried to. Yet some poems appearing in the mix feel like they were expressing my 'true self' coming through the whole time. A good example is "Polarity," the first poem in this series, and the earliest, written in June of 2009, right after graduating high school, while out of my urban environment visiting my aunt, uncle, and cousins in Bellingham, Massachusetts, surrounded by nature. It's the type of poem I wrote without completely grasping what I was symbolizing, and one I find I understand better over time.

Writing helped me see that it is wishful thinking to expect anyone to accompany us on the adventure of life (but understandable to hope for it) in the way we imagine them to be; to be something they aren't for us, as well as us for them, when our road is our own. To love someone or something and ourselves enough to let go, even when we want to pull them closer when we should not. To accept a journey in each of us that is alone, even if we are together in that loneliness, whether or not we are next to, holding hands, having sex, laughing, crying or talking with a person we love. It's a hard pill to swallow.

Writing also helped me see that it is wishful thinking to expect anyone or anything to hand us Truth on a silver platter— that Truth is not so much something given by pure revelation as it is a series of revelations arrived at by hard work, reflection and study.

The spiritual, intellectual, and political themes cannot be separated from my immediate environment, such as my family and my household (which features exclusively in one of the poems) and growing up in the most urban part of Elizabeth, New Jersey (the most densely populated state in the country),[3] with New York City as a stomping ground, always just a short train ride away. All my struggles, internal and external, took place in this setting and are inevitably colored by it.

My love for music and song lyrics has always been a major poetic inspiration for me. But although I am a music fanatic and a drummer, I do not count the rhythm when I write, I feel it out; I prefer improvisation and then refinement, usually letting a rhythm or image find its way out of me, even if what is expressed is

---

[3] My high school graduating class was over 900 students.

discombobulated or there isn't much of a consistent rhyme or rhythm at first. I rework it later if I'm aiming for a desired effect, something clearer or something deliberately vague. Most of my poems are conceived of as chunky blocks of marble that are then chipped away at, to various degrees, over the course of time.

Finally, I should note that while compiling this volume I was reading mystical Middle Eastern poetry, particularly Kahlil Gibran and Rumi, which inspired me to experiment with *rubaiyat*. As well as William Blake and certain alchemical texts, such as the infamous *Corpus Hermeticum,* and various other esoteric texts from which I have drawn conceptual language, such as P.D. Ouspensky, G.I. Gurdjieff and Carlos Castaneda. In their footsteps, I began to view writing in general, and especially my poetic exercises, as reflective and spiritual acts of self-study, much like the Sufis. Like Rumi, longing and loss was the initial motivation for my verses, the wellspring of poets throughout the ages, and from this fountain the rest flowed.

Overall, the poems progressively hone in on a battle to learn and acquire knowledge while here in this crazy, tumultuous experience of living, in this time and place, as a human with the hand he's been dealt—bouncing between complete despair and boundless joy for the mystery of it all. These poems are pictures of the pain and joy that accompanies being graced with even just a drop of *gnosis*, of trying to understand our existence here from the bowels of a concrete jungle through consistent effort. To *bear witness* is the least I could do while living in the heart of an empire, with dwindling leg space and elbow room, and a whole world to explore, as a wanderlust-filled pauper trapped in debt-slavery, always with the feeling that someday might be too late to explore and learn all that I wished to. Putting together this book was a step towards less feeling hopeless and sorry for myself, and more action—more doing. To give back to others. To relinquish my fears. To be heard.

Putting *knowledge*, its application and distribution, over all else as *the path to Love* became my goal, and I saw that only knowledge could reveal to us how to truly love objectively—to give back—to see the Words of Cosmic Mind, of God, and attempt to read what Nature has to say, what science, literature, and human history has to say, and what is unsaid, what is erased from it or hidden that must be excavated! To gather and sift through information and to watch our surroundings, ourselves, each other, to analyze and observe why we believe what we do and grow together, is the highest act of Love. We, as individuals, are a similar maze to explore—a whole world—to study not apart from the earth's history and the universe, but alongside them. Loving something is seeing it for what it is, using discernment. Each experience, relationship, friendship, acquaintance, and moment holds a lesson to behold that we may try to identify. Poetry can assist in capturing the lesson while we are undergoing its wrath, the pain we suffer to gain wisdom.

Through much encouragement (and some pressure) over the years, I feel I should finally share some of these personal writings in print. How wonderful it is to be a part of such magic! The beauty of literature, of the word, of having a strewn out conversation with the living and the dead, my old friends! And how horrifyingly liberating to see the symbol as a key to both deception and to unlocking our internal and external reality. Of excavating the Truth hidden inside of us and society as a whole, despite the word's ability to also bury it in fruitless arguments, its frequent regression into a "distressing vanity"[4] without revelation, or to be used as an outright tool for manipulation. A tool for both war and wisdom.

Words are part of the *labyrinth* through which we must labor to understand, to extricate ourselves from our prisons of ignorance.

---

[4] Fulcanelli, *Le Mystère des Cathédrales: Esoteric Interpretation of the Hermetic Symbols of the Great Work,* trans. Mary Sworder, (Las Vegas, Nevada: Brotherhood of Light, Inc. 1984), 43.

We are *"the Word made flesh"*, the very *speaking* of *"kun fayakūn"*. We are *living symbols, living words*, of which our myths and gods, our numbers and sciences, and our written and spoken languages, were only ever reflections. Just as we are the reflections—the numbers, gods, goddesses, verbs, adjectives, nouns, metaphors and similes—of an eternal Cosmic Mind.

How vulnerable I am in your hands now, yet my mind has flown to *you!* You hold pictures of its thoughts, emotions, habits, experiences, and bits of things learned along the way. You hold a piece of it, as *another version of me in One Head looking at Your(Its)self.* I hope my little word paintings unlock something inside of you, too, both personally and impersonally transcendent.

The Author,
Elizabeth, New Jersey,
March 24, 2015

Polarity

O' the fortunes, they can speak
and those Lions can roar!
To those who seek
to hear more
and see
One.

For
each one,
there are many.
Aspects of every side,
opinions that fluster plenty.
Stars apart within a great divide.

Light that Accrues

In what I drink with eyes as I am
among those that lift my hand,
I see arcane birds of prey
watching my refusal to obey.
Feet are bound in cement,
forcing me down into descent
as the water rises to my nose
for the very struggle to oppose.
Will I find comfort in the blue,
in the reflecting Light that accrues?
Or can I really stay on the shore
with someone here to be there for?
If the air I am fed refreshes me,
if I find joy in all that I see,
could this shift the polarity?
Could I keep this Light, this Sea,
sailing forward, to be me?

Passive Face

A smile, so brief I can feel it fade.
It dwindles down to a passive face;
its departure seems like a decade.
That moment has passed; it feels erased.

I wish that every second perceived
was filled with that laughter there.
With him
sitting on the grass, my mind relieved,
yet a brief rendition of despair.
Naïve.

I cannot stop the thought from fleeing:
I am fooling myself into falsehood.
That every hint I think I am seeing
is just one more thing misunderstood.

That Temperance Torn

Charade of acquisition,
intake of symbols and sounds.
Borrowed ideas, capital calculation,
forests of restless hounds.
Incognito walks an outsider
watching the matter unfold.
Alone, hidden in skin, rising higher,
bearing stories told.
Fists are balled-up spheres,
retaining solitude and scorn,
as he curses himself,
all of his fears

in that temperance torn.

Bliss for Me to Deny

Why do I sit and dwell in-between the smiles?
A belying gesture, an invisible crutch in you,
which I will not speak of beyond all these miles.
I can tread right beside, yet my distance persists.
My mind is always within and confined to
the flustering of misunderstood glances amiss.
Let me be! Steal that Sun from the sky!
I always hope to see it, yet it fills me with duality
in equal amounts dread and bliss for me to deny.
Why do I even yearn to be seen in those rays?
I continue under the reflecting rock malady,
hiding in its dim light as I drift through the days.

One Moon, No Sun, and Ten of Swords

A man stumbling alone in the dark,
drunk on the shores of Assateague Island,
on the brink of falling and fading.
Ocean City lights, Ferris wheel, boardwalk
protruding in the distance.
He never left that night of absent light,
all joy fleeting, vision pervading.
Who will discover his body lying there
facedown in the blood-soaked sand?
Ten swords protruding from his back,
pinning him down, placed by his own hand.
Luna drags the tides to meet
that dank face, skeletal with his despair.
Every grain will gather to bring him home,
to bury those eyes of which he thought:
no one cared.

The light of the Star overlooked them
as it continued on its way to the other side.
So the man buried their gaze in the sand
to conceal with the seas that they had cried.

15

Only Dreaming

I
gasp.
Grasping
this ethereal
spade, chipping
away at the soil un-
controllably. Sink a little
lower; mentally pervade. Why
does my grip tighten desperately?
Why does this luminosity vanish from
perspective? Pull it closer, yet feel further
away. All that is seen are walls rising over me
as I dig a little deeper. Am I objective? I think I
forgot my rope above or below. There's no one
willing to toss it up or down. Just keep digging,
to what do I owe? That light overhead just
dwindles now. It is shrinking down to
insignificance as
I forget the concept
of meaning. I maintain a
virulent constant vigilance,
although it is dark and I am only

dreaming.

Looking back on these words,
I call a spade a spade.
Seeking alone, yet longing for you.

Burning this Fear

See the Star rise again, its light casting joy.
How the rays warm me and extinguish the void,
replacing a shadow with desire to employ.
Yet as it descends behind that horizon vast,
I am sinking again; into a great abyss I relapse.
No color within sight. No more light to cast.
All I can do is sit in the dark and wait…
for the fortified fixation to return to me, negate
the imbalance inside, internally conflate!
Bright Star, my desire, please return to me here
so I may rekindle that wondrous warmth to revere.
Expelling this darkness. Burning this fear.

Molten Sea

Wearing a sun around the neck,
Horus's Eye,
he fears never having it to hold on trek.

A Moon reflects off of his skin,
yet does not illuminate enough within.
As he waits for one to explode, in rebirth die,
he hopes the other falls from the sky.

to sustain him

      waiting to get closer

      He wants to jump inside,
      let the flames sear away the pride,
      sink to the bottom and walk on the core,
      bringing the Moon with him to adore.

      Going circular in that molten sea,
      swimming laps in the rays for an eternity.

No Light of My Own

How can something so cold make energy of its own?
Doing circles in the dark does not mean progression.
And I really have no light, yours is all I have known.
The racing rays reveal me to myself, to all things.
They illuminate my face in the night so I can see me
and brighten that stone heart until is soars and sings.
Hanging in the sky with no light of my own, I wait
for something greater than me to take my place,
to carry its warmth to my surface, in me sedate
my restless mind and lifeless surface, exempt from air.
An amiable disposition for the cosmos to gaze upon,
a realization that without you I was never there.

Slice of Tides

Each
moment
a slice of
cycles vaster than you,
despite the individual view.
Each pair of eyes, seen or unseen,
existing in you,
we in a dream,
or so it seems.

Though this I do know:
when I stare at each face,
I see only 'me,' in various forms,
a cornucopia of shapes.

Each mouth, a vibration
carrying out the Verb(s) of God(s),
in splitting, transitory façades.
Each frequency flourishing apart;
Black, White, Red—restart,
into the spinning, electric Art!
Dendritic and fractal,
together, apart.

Though this I do feel:
when I close my eyes,
I live only as us inside
of tides

every slice inside

we are the closed and open eyes

Up a Mountain & Down a Stream

Up a mountain,
the evolution of a human
surrounded by our self-destruction.
A hard plight;
a mental precipice; no road ahead
to guide us through this endless f(l)ight
that scars the ego, exiled.

Down a stream
of consciousness and dreams
surrounded by boughs and beams.
A sacred bark;
a heartstring river; rows of trees
gliding past with raised arms to mark
the journey home.

How Do I Detach From...? (A Dialogue with...)

How
could I ever possibly solidify You
into pictures or words?
In what fashion?
In what way
that does not impose,
that does not breed herds?

Do I
speak to a 'being' in me
who is *not* a part of me?
Outside of me?
One I am not composed of?
In what way
that does not attach,
that does not restrain we?

Detach
myself from the I's inside
and there *I* find final Truth.
On a path,
I need not force it.
I simply tread
Your roots.

From
all and nothing is Your face;
material notions
only replicate Your grace.
They must never take Your place.
We are You, playing these roles.
Genuflection to the Master Mind!
How do I play the role of
facing infinity without flinching?

Brewed

Sip and inhale
these shades in-between:
sitting in that moment there
at university, in front of the library
with a cup, a conclusion at the butt,
as my ass freezes on this metal chair.
Smooth, warm liquid lavishly flows
down into my stomach, churning,
a luscious, strong, calming complexion.
Our lives intermingle
within a cup of joe,
blackened beans—white, steamed
creamy overflow.
Sweetened bitterness.
Like a cigarette, guiltily lit
with a dark core, dressed
in white sheath. Life's grey areas:
that fire set to disintegrate.
Savoring the dark tones in a daze,
always with a lighter saccharine blaze.
All that's left is to take the last gulp,
the final smoke;
staring at Katz's grey hair and glasses,
clouds passing overhead
with glorious insight.
Living is never just black,
never just white.
In incubation, I brood.

Triple Disaster

'9.0 earthquake in Japan' flies by
on my screen. Online newsfeed.
Click. Read: ...*Tsunami*
                warning.

        I walk out of my room to see
the scenes on TV,
        as waves sweep away
cars in afternoon traffic,
        houses in heaps like toys
                at the beach.   Screams out of reach.
        Ships float through the streets,
sucked under bridges.
        Thousands die in minutes
as I am safe under this roof.

Returning to my room,
        those cars on repeat in my mind.
                I cry.

Called a best friend to
check up on another friend
in Yokohama;
she was on the safer end
of the island. She felt the earthquake.
        Nuclear meltdowns
shortly after—no one was ever 'safe,'
        at least not anymore.
        A triple disaster.

Ruled by the Numbers

Many stumble around chasing paper.
Another tangible thing: temporary thrill,
another distraction to make us feel safer.
You, object user and object breaker,
why not lift the power of the green bill?
Many stumble around chasing paper.
Truth: the only measure of inch and acre.
Pleasant lies in the mind, swallow a blue pill:
another distraction to make us feel safer.
Does 'more expensive' make you greater?
Pursuit of wealth snuffs knowledge and skill!
Many stumble around chasing paper
in a maze of forgery, fraud, and fakers,
who would do anything for *the numbers*—even kill!
Another distraction to make us feel safer:
flip on the TV, become a green paper crusader,
for the new deals and false-hope 'free will.'
Many stumble around chasing paper,
another distraction to make us feel safer.

Break the form!
Ruled by the numbers
with only *gnosis* to set us free,
yet never certainty.
Take a risk,
fall in Love with uncertainty

27

Food for the Fed

I
hide
the Truth.
Manufacture
poison with smiles
and consent. Free energy
for none—they are the human-
fuel and souls spent for servitude
and rent. Debt: your whips and chains.
Budget cuts line my mansions with sparkling
blood, like the rubies on my fingers—diamond studs.
The path I tread is laid with the dead: *inflation* and *interest*

makes them food for the Fed!

Inflating the chickens
before the slaughter,
for selfish interests.

What I am really?
Predator's Mind
Demiurge

Percussion

Hands are tools
for cognitive projections—reactions,
     dancing on rhythms of emotions.
Fervent fingers rumble with branches
             gliding across skin, a gust of wind,
tearing through the leaves on our crown in a raging fit of passion,
or breezing up our spine
caressing the heart

subtly.

Dynamic like the weather—suddenly!
     Crackling!
     Fierce lightning, encores of thunderous roars,
         shaking our being
         to its core.

Hands are tools.
       Soul is what makes them
              soar (sore).

Heirs

Remnants of the past strewn about
as the heirs brush past them, shrouded
in amnesia,
in REM sleep.

Forgetting sapiens stumble in the dark,
too arrogant in their own ways
to see.

Great feats of masonry,
signs and numbers on pages of flora and fauna,
do hide the mystery
inside of us.

Great minds strewn across,
most wasting away,
an array abundant hoarding in dishonesty.
Few *remember*.

Equiprimordial

Formative Matrix
Blackness is each particle and wave,
macro and micro; there, yet not there
—nothing and the potential for everything.

Great Mother, *Templo Corporis*, Womb of all time,
I am your veil lifted; truth is in *mind*
and *heart* combined.
Humbly, fearlessly ambivalent, shall I return
to your ebony arms of sky.

Father, Son and Lover of Sophia, seed of my being,
I am your face in small; I seek heart
guiding the mind, *defined*.
In joy and suffering I give.
The I is gone in the blink of an eye.
She will remain.

White Light of the Black One, gracing all forms,
micro and macro; not there, yet there
—shape and motion expanding.
Seeded Seedling seeding Thought

An Ever-Changing View

Confusion takes hold like a blackout,
    putrefying period of personal transition,
yet sometimes so dependent
        on one of the other versions of ourselves existing.
Walking about as separate minds in One Head
    with that need to share our bodies and thoughts,
to take risks in unraveling each other instead.
        Failures will seem impervious,
no matter how clever, bold, witty,
    spiritually aware or well-read;
you, too, will encounter this darkness and dread.
        Mirrors rise and shatter,
on and on, reflecting new parts of yourself
    while destroying others, left to scatter.
Some faces go away, some only temporarily,
        while others change positions
beyond recognition necessarily.
        And then some appear like intimate apparitions,
so suddenly and subtly,
        in a single moment of like-minded energy.
Yet no matter where our paths cross or diverge,
    each one is forever and always a part of you,
despite this physical realm,
        with its ever-changing view.

33

To Give and to Receive

Force imbued in a thing
form among forms
of Form
Shape of a Seed
spiraling and expanding
Ellipsis and infinite axes
rotating, transcending
ejaculating energy
descending

Force recoils from a thing
blacker than the blackest
blackness.
Shape of Shapelessness
decaying womb
of emergence
passive
infinite silence
resting potentiality
awaiting
ascension

Dancing *Now*here Altogether

Eyes zoom in
    like a lens, fixating
        on pink petals seeping
through,
    emerging from barky shell.

They seem so still, yet are
    in constant motion, growing,
too slightly to see.

    An I immersed
in a portal of pigment,
    a single   petal,
trying   to   penetrate profoundly
    into the molecules;
     to move with them.

I read
    the same
       language:
            LVX.
  Dancing
    *Now*here
        Altogether.
    Yet each
on our
    (its) own,
        a Word.

35

Stumbling into Battle

Here I am, invoking *You* again.
But I *am* You—made *of* You—I live through You,
so do I invoke me? I do not yet know myself.
I need your help, my Friend!
I am so lost,
with no lover now but You.
Meditation, study, exploration, experimentation, prayer—
they can be the same, right?
What am I supposed to learn from all of this?
What would Rumi say to me right now?
That I am a drunkard?
That I am searching in the darkness?
More often than not it feels like stumbling
rather than marching
forward into battle.
To battle, nonetheless!
I am of the Lion's Den!

So I look up.

These stars are so beautiful!
We are like these stars.
Immortal in relative perspective,
yet soon to be extinguished,
transfigured, a memory in a Mind,

36

to scatter into 'new' material,
reaching further out and
in, to forms unfathomable
yet already there, here, somewhere—
conceived of, waiting to become—
something! How vague.
Dr. Rich would tell me to fly my helicopter
down to an object of affection,
but I like to fly it up and then down again.
Besides, my muse has departed.

So I look in.

Where do I go from here?
The most-asked question in history!
It certainly is beautiful, though…
living, that is.
Whatever that is.
Whatever *this* is.
It is.

Horrifying, mysterious, and sublime,
a battlefield that leaves us shaking.
A river flowing through the body rind,
perpetually breathgiving and breathtaking.

Grains in a Demitasse

Bodies, beautiful and distracting!
Alarmingly enticing, fascinating—
often repulsive to the seeking mind.
Perhaps I should not think too much
about this servant of the creator
and his beautiful form.
A free man, whose mind and flesh bring me comfort,
but whose heart is guarded as I guard my own.
His face reminds me of my former lover's,
but his eyes are his own and his kiss tastes different,
a birthmark on his lip.
An intriguing book I have never read;
the cover drawing me in to explore the contents.
I open my book. He opens his. We both read.
Why should this hurt?
I knew what I was getting myself into.
'Moving on'
moves us into strange places.
I know what he wants.
I wanted it, too,
but more…

Pleasures of the flesh, what lessons do you teach?
Do I seek comfort in you when I should seek it
in solitude,
in the spinning of the Cosmos, the Beloved?
The idea of budding again frightens me!

38

Wishful thinking! Expectations, a curse.
How can I take back my mind?
And where do I draw the line?
How much is *too much*?
Abstinence or temperance?
Do I keep the heart confined,
just please the flesh, move on?
To wait.
"The secrets of the truth won't be revealed
through asking too many questions,"[5] Rumi says.
Questioning questions, questions overflow the head,
and verses. Talking in questions, my natural verse.
Verses flow. I disperse.
I'm not fifty yet, but my heart and eyes are bloody.
"From all this talk, no one finds the way to ecstasy."[6]

I wish I could just whirl like a dervish
forever.
Losing my Shams of Tabriz,
walking around a pillar,
spewing verses in longing.
To understand
directly experiencing *to be*
forgetting the strife *to become,* but feeling it,
knowing it,
embodying the Cosmos in one single body.
And then come back. Know a body,
know another, know, know…
know
love.

---

[5] Kabir Helminski, ed. and trans., *The Pocket Rumi,* (Boston, MA: Shambhala Publications, Inc., 2001), Rubaiyat 1088, 13-14.
[6] Ibid, 14.

No ledge. I live on a precipice I am in love with;
to expect anyone else to follow, to dance here with me,
contradicts my lessons.
"Not everyone's a philosopher," free man reminds me.
He's right.

But where is my Shams Tabrizi?
Could such profound love ever find me?
I wonder if Rumi would approve of this lust,
of how I find it hard to distinguish it anymore;
can it not be a spiritual experience, a lesson of its own?
A different type of union than what I knew before?
Is it worth it to explore? I grow weary on the shore.
Has *our* chapter truly ended?
This man is still a page, not a chapter,
as far as I can tell, yet the future
bends.
Is it too much to want someone who *sees*?
Is it 'wrong' to sometimes settle to simply please?

To understand love,
to not possess another, but let them be,
to let myself and another be free
through knowledge.
Free to choose where to place our hearts and minds.
Whatever that means...
What do I even mean?
What is free? Gurdjieff says in my head. *'Choose?'*
You talk theory, but do not really grasp.

How do we grow without being true mirrors?
Pointing out what is possible to work on, accepting
what isn't, and that only each of us,
on our own,

can do what is necessary to *love gnosis*—
learn to love learning,
to love knowing in order to know love
—self-study—
the first step to freeing ourselves!
To know 'God'?
On our own, yes,
yet in order to do it
we need mirrors to point out our blind spots,
not as Nemesis
pointing Narcissus to his reflection
and sending him to his death.
Yet getting to the point of even acknowledging
the notion and possibility
that we are imprisoned in flesh, in ego uncontrolled but used
as a remote-controller, in body slavery with more than one body,
psychologically manipulated, constantly bombarded
by signals and triggers—
that we do not *choose* anything—
'Hey, this way… no, this way… this… pay attention to this,'
often so subtle we do not even sense it
—just that, alone,
is an incredible leap that many would not willingly dive into!
The difference between intellectually knowing one is a 'machine'
as opposed to truly feeling it, even for just a moment.
We cannot act for another, only point.
No one can act for us, only point.
How terrifying! How to distinguish when pointing
is productive and when it is manipulative?
That is active love, G. said.
'Point where?' the Sun asks whenever I quoted G.
'You're too vague.'
I could hardly explain such a *seeing*,
for I can hardly control an inch of my own being.

41

That is as far as I have come, that admitting.
How can I solidify this perspective
into these sounds and squiggles!
Philo Sophia! Love, knowledge, and wisdom as *one thing*, eternal,
encompassing all possibilities, predatory to symbiotic—
discernment:
where do you place your energy?
Do you really have control of that placement,
or do you tell yourself you do?
Different 'you's', G. said.
This one just wanted an escape
for a little while
from pressure,
not being with *him*,
my romantic love unrequited
to a suffering friend,
done with 'school' for a while,
time to get a job,
finish a damn book,
carry my family!
Free man was a vacation.

But I remain here, in a perspective lived, unyielding.
Not a Buddha, Muhammad, or Jesus, but a seeker.
Could I ever find my compliment on this invisible ledge?
Who would dance with me on this cliff?
So much time wasted on the fear of being alone.
So much circumlocution!
Machine! G. yelled in my head, an itch wedging into my actions,
with his strange habit of 'being right'…
I lacked the control I was writing about.
I could at least glimpse it now.
Stop seeking another—pursue your own purpose!
Don't wallow over him or anyone;

read, meditate, write, drum, paint, go out, grow stronger, teach!
But this coffee is so good, damn it!
A taste won't hurt; I had to prove it to myself—I am my own Sun.
It doesn't have to be *him* or free man; it could be anyone.
When least expected, they could come.
Seek knowledge and they may arrive in due time.
Or not. Should it matter either way? We live and die alone.
Be like Yunus Emre on the last line,
remind myself at the end of each verse:
Daniel, *"make not complaint that you have suffering*
known because of Love;
All that is needful for the lovers comes to them
from the Beloved."[7]
But then why is Turkish delight so
delightful?
Would the Beloved deny me a chance to taste?
My choice! Or is it?
He is within that Beloved as much as I,
any lack of control over himself or I a part of This Mind,
so the Beloved calls out to me: 'Move on, and give it a try!'
live this moment, learn this lesson,
with a footnote: 'Just remember to not overindulge,
pay attention to why. Don't lie to yourself!'

You could place this energy elsewhere, G. said.
For now, all you can do is collect data, self-study;
change is not yet possible.

Ibn Al-'Arabi warned me:
"So preserve yourselves, my brothers,
from the calamities of this place,

---

[7] Süha Faiz trans., *City of the Heart: Yunus Emre's Verses of Wisdom and Love*, (Rockport, MA: Element Books Limited, 1992), 16.

for distinguishing it is extremely difficult!
Souls find it sweet, and then within it they are duped,
since they become completely enamored of it."[8]
Here, in these bodies, trying to collect lessons!
I am as easily duped and enamored as the next seeker
on his path, in this urban jungle.
Of course, at my age,
this was the easiest thing to become enamored of.

After finishing our coffee,
free man told me to place my saucer over the demitasse,
spin it three times, flip it over, and let it sit.
We talked with the record player in the background,
Rolling Stones, passion while flipping the record, then a movie.
Before laying down to sleep, he lifted the demitasse
and told me what he saw in the grains:
faces and trees;
people in my life or people who may enter it;
a forest and a wise old man with a stone.
Tarot #9, I thought. *My kismet!*
I did not get any sleep that night
next to someone who wasn't *him*,
as much of a delight as free man was.
He fell asleep right away.
"The heart and the mind
are left angry with each other."[9]
Because I cannot sleep I read Rumi
until the sun greeted me through the curtains.
It was not *him* anymore….
Temperance was letting go;
so should I.

---

[8] Sufi Shaykh, Ibn Al-'Arabi, in Futuhat (Unveiling) III 38.23, translated and quoted by William Chittick in *The Sufi Path of Knowledge*, 263.
[9] Helminski, *Pocket Rumi*, Ghazels, "Because I Cannot Sleep," 58.

How do I aspire like the falcon, be prideful like the leopard,
and victorious in my times of war?
Guile like a serpent?
"Don't get too involved
with the nightingale and the peacock.
One is all words and the other all colors."[10]
Which one is which?

Free man and I eventually met up again,
in the tryst that was once a safe haven
for my former-lover and I.
This room is no longer special between us.

"In perplexity the fear of failure and the
hope of success
always are in conflict with each other,
advancing, retreating."[11]

I know this perplexity flows from You!
All of it has only ever been You,
the only one I could count on.
Teaching me to see the *Centre*
of my centers; to seek discipline, control, will.

"I was constantly involved with ambition,
and now he tells me to break all the chains."[12]

Easier said than done!
G. said in my head.

---

[10] *Pocket Rumi*, Rubaiyat 1078, 13.
[11] *Pocket Rumi*, Mathnawi VI, 203-11, 252.
[12] *Pocket Rumi*, Rubaiyat 1129, 15.

To a Midnight Mistress and a Golden Bird, Together in the Information War

Two sisters I never had
greet me at my door,
and I at theirs.
Worlds transformed.

She walked into Katz's class
on generations of American Literature
(we walked out as the next batch).
Baggy clothes, a didgeridoo.
Deepest of discussions.
All the odd mystical shit floating around the net.
The internet, Indra's Net and Maya's Veil.
She loved a golden bird
who I actually met once before, through *him*.
Talk of politics, conspiracies, UFOs,
consciousness, spirituality, evil,
war crimes, poetry, literature,
nature, the beauty of green,
all the protesting across the globe,
trying to eat clean
yet hardly anything left
untainted.
Smoking in the sun, laying on the grass.
She never wore makeup or flashy jewelry,
and didn't show off her body.
She loved to dance. She loved to love.
Never seemed to care much if others saw her as odd.
We opened up to each other as lovers do.

The beginning of marches in Manhattan.
Making last minute signs (without her the first time)

on pieces of cardboard in another friend's car—
*"It is no measure of health to be well adjusted
to a profoundly sick society."* –Jiddu Krishnamurti
Missed the morning march,
but found a golden bird at the park
that night, September 17.
Stood with a sign, people stopping and staring,
some laughing, most glancing or ignoring,
some yelling,
some reading, some talking to you.
Dr. MLK in my ear all year: proudly maladjusted!
My mistress and I singing that one Arcade Fire song
on the road to Newark Penn Station.
More 'occupying!'
Whatever the hell it was—
I was never quite sure, and always aware of that.
A spectator. A camera.
Meditations in a golden bird's nest in Jersey City.
Singing songs, drumming on anything, singing bowls.
Talk of 'the future.' An *ancient stone!*
A looming feeling of boots pressing on our necks!
DEBT!!! Cataclysms?
The evil in humanity—*what is it?*
If you camp out for a new iPhone, you're a good consumer.
Camp out against depravity, oppression, imperialism, militarism,
fascism, racism, and apartheid—
you're 'disrupting the peace'! How ironic!
'Put that conscience away, son,
I don't have time for it.'
'So what's your one demand?' they asked. Different answers,
different people. I watched. Symptoms of something greater.
How do we have 'one demand' or 'one cause'
when each issue is systematically interconnected?
Lots of bitching, yet not enough studying and finger-lifting.
And people just trying to get to work,
some shouting:
'Get a fucking job!'
'Fucking liberals… democrats… leftists…
conspiracy theorists…

communists… hippies….'
Oracle Orwell interjection:
"And even when they became discontented,
as they sometimes did, their discontent led nowhere,
because being without general ideas,
they could only focus in on petty specific grievances.
The larger evils invariably escaped their notice."
How can we possibly escape it?
How do the greater evils escape so many?
Petty specific grievances galore,
some getting closer to the core.
I was there, with the mistress and the golden bird,
and many others; various causes,
one microphone.
Some fighting,
some just trying to understand,
some taking advantage, fiends and media spin.
I saw brothers, sisters,
the homeless, mentally ill, and disabled,
students, professors, parents, grandparents,
many colors and creeds,
former soldiers, 9/11 first responders,
an underqualified-overqualified degree spectrum,
the employed and the unemployed,
illegal immigrants (American history!),
poets, musicians, photographers, designers, dancers, actors,
journalists, celebrities,
that Michael Moore guy and Tim Robbins—random!
Hippies, hipsters, fad following frolicking
confusion. A new trend.
A lifestyle. A passion.
An old one in a new form.
Tents and computer bases at Zuccotti Park
(and around the country)
for an information war
in digital trenches,
psychological arm wrestling,
social media explosion,
newspapers and bullhorns

shouting at the Wall Street bull.
Calling out their bullshit.
Community feasts of free food.
Generous givers and lying leeches.
Dancing and drum circles.
Acidheads.
Various types of conservatives
and various types of radicals.
Socialists, Democrats, Democratic Socialists, Anarchists….
I found I could relate to none, yet to all.
Still hung up on the zeitgeist and technology,
planned obsolescence, the banking cartels.
I knew there was a deeper cause than the external symptoms,
I thought it was the monetary system,
'fractional reserve banking'
(a major factor regardless)
not yet seeing the true Face of Evil:
pathological personalities
by nature
in disguises,
who maintain that system.
Tygers and Lambs; nature and nurture;
Names of God.
Lions in the jungle—
all I could do was nudge the herd!
Look out!

It microcosmed at university.
Campus life discontent.
President Fraudhi's mask slips. Exposed.
Campus corporatocracy.
We marched to some pointless senator's office,
only about a hundred of us.
Left our signs in front. Captured on YouTube Land.
A few of us sleeping in tents, 'occupying'
with my midnight mistress.
Between the University Center and Starbucks.
Wet grass, sleeping bags. Lots of staring.
Scorned, laughed at, turned away from,

praised by the teacher's union.
Talked to a few people.
Learned the lot of life lessons.
Mini-politics, global reflection.
'You scratch my back, I'll scratch yours
or else...'
Fuck integrity, "the policy only applies to students."
Cliché euphemisms for hard truths.
And euphemisms for departments "phased out."
Eventually, I see the predator's den.
You lie or defend a liar
and get a promotion,
a scholarship, and so on.
Not reprimanded—a bonus!
Aesthetics, appearances > academic content, integrity.
I stayed up past midnight with the mistress.
We awoke, contents of our tents,
right across from the CAS building.
One of my strangest memories.
Fuck what everyone thought! Liberating.
All I had to do was cross a patch of grass to get to class.
Sleeping on campus is convenient.
Who needs a dorm room when you've got lawns?
A mysterious woman greeted us in the morning,
her hair cut short, wearing a long fur coat
(not sure if it was 'real,' though).
She had a heavy bag of Dunkin Donuts and coffee
in a giant cardboard box with a drain.
She said she could not give us her name.
Told us years ago she helped sway the vote
for the president to get his job.
Trying to save face—what a strange experience...
Connected to the (chess)Board of 'Trust'ees
and administration.
Brought the coffee and donuts as a gesture of goodwill.
Wished more people cared
about the ostensibly radical (ridiculous) acts
we enacted at this school we knew could be so much more.
She wished she could do more.

51

(Many jobs were on the line)
Guilt in her eyes, in her voice.
She actually cried.
The midnight-haired mistress and I knew
that this entire experience
alone,
made all of our shouting
worth its weight in gold!

Poetry class. Writing about writing.
Questioning where we were going,
why we even write at all.
A golden bird who scribbled dreamy verses,
sang songs. Cleverly dressed. Feminine, beautiful yet
reserved. Gentle, yet firm. Mysterious. Intelligent. Caring.
Strong beautiful soul, like the mistress.
We whispered to each other in our seats and laughed.
Some people thought we were 'together.'
Started pretending to be for fun.
She danced with her words as she read them on stage.
A bird who protested and shouted them, too,
her hymns for a new habitat.
Savorer of books,
grass, trees, forests, bees—
gathering *gnosis*, churning it.
I saw how easily one could fall in love with this bird.
We graduated together, her on one side of me,
he on the other—uncanny!
Wrote an essay about a lot of this;
received a scholarship from the teacher's union.
Hardly anyone was there, not even him.
Katz and Diaz rushed in last minute
before my speech.
Two endings that month, bitter sweet.
Now that those years are lived,

I see that my professors,
he,
the bird and mistress,
all the interesting encounters
in that cougar's den
lifted me up—
listened to all of my oddities.
We shared our burdens without snobbery.
We learned our lessons as commodities.
We entered each other's stories,
wrote them together.
We are written
with stars.

My mistress and the bird are mothers now,
as I always saw them.
Androgynous embodiments
of Divine Femininity!
I think now:
Each with a fresh new mind to tend to,
to equip for an information war. A predatory world.
I shuddered....
Yet in this whole frightening existence,
still I think:
those sure are some lucky babies
to come from such women
who did not just exist,
but *lived*
to be heard!

"Through the darkness
we shall illuminate."
    —a golden bird

Eaten by the Salary

Morning to debt servitude
via railways.
A feeble woman crouched over,
sitting on the filthy stairs
of the Elizabeth Train Station,
a Broad Street scent concoction
of food and urine in the air.
Her face is covered
by her bent knees;
arm dangles, draped
over the steps with a hand stuffed
in a bag of potato chips,
motionless.
A cup of Dunkin Donuts coffee
sits beside her purse on the steps,
the concrete ground covered
in black spots
of old chewing gum.
She is frozen,
a pillar of salt,
perhaps eaten by the salary,
by the spirits,
or CIA heroin.
This is what "America runs on…"
We are old chewing gum
discarded.

I wondered
what was her story?

The Screen

Days are colder,
mid-October.
Tighten the scarf.
Standing on the platform,
waiting for the train.
Hone in on a man.
Brown hat, grey hair, jean jacket,
glasses. His eyes glued
to a cellphone screen,
like the man on each side of him.
Glance up and down the platform.
On every bench,
each with a 'smart' phone
in their hand, staring back at them;
little girls and elderly men,
all colored collars,
with brown hats and denim jackets,
not looking at each other.
I dug into my pocket,
wrapped my hand around it,
and thought...

Lying in Bed

"A day without blood is like a day without sunshine."
The TV was still on in the next room as I awoke.
Grabbed my phone: nearly 8 AM.
My father had never gone to sleep;
he'll sleep through the afternoon.
I wanted to go back to sleep and sleep into it.
But I could hear the movie Full Metal Jacket on again,
in the living room—he watched this movie incessantly,
even putting it on last Christmas,
which upset everyone in the room, yet he was oblivious.
How festive.
His twitching seemed to get worse, his paranoia immense,
threatened by having to be taken care of by *me* in the future
rather than by my grandmother, who carried all of us.
The little pride in himself he had left
dwindled at this prospect: that I no longer needed him,
but he needed me to survive longer in this world.
His desperation for praise and reassurance evident
each time he said "I'm making ____ tonight."
"You like ____, right?"
even if it was a meal he had been cooking me for years;
he *needed* to ask me if I 'liked it,' everyday
(even when it was the unhealthiest meal he could make).
Sometimes I just didn't respond, or with an irritated "yeah, sure."
It seems such a petty thing to get irritated by…
Sometimes I don't know how to speak to him at all—
being around him too long puts you on edge.
He's going deaf. He repeats himself.

You always wind up raising your voice
because he spoke so loudly.
His hair was always disheveled,
and he wore the same kind of white undershirt and jeans,
hardly ever anything else,
no need to express himself in appearances beyond that.
Being diagnosed with dyslexia growing up
in a school system that did not yet have programs catered
to any learning disabilities, certainly didn't help,
nor did having a father who walked out before he was a teenager,
or a schizophrenic brother
(my uncle, who died upstairs when I was ten).
Nor did the bottle, and constantly staring into the TV.
Only gardening in our little patch of land helped him,
and his life was better than most people in his shoes
especially because of his mother.
Even if assisted, he still did what he could
with what he had—our little garden, the perfect example;
an important lesson to pass on to a son.
He could tell the weather by looking at the sky,
possessed street smarts, and had stories to tell.
But as I lay here, I pitied my parents and hated myself for it.
My mom angrily bickered with him, as usual,
as he teased her incessantly, as usual,
repeating dirty lines from Full Metal Jacket to annoy her.
"Me so horny, me love you long time."
"SHUT UUUUP!!!" she bellowed,
never any consideration that anyone else might still be sleeping,
or trying to go back to sleep. I have no work today.
"What's wrong with that guy, huh?"
"Would you stop it!" she shouts.
"What's wrong with him, huh? Why's he turning white?"
"Turn it off, you motherfucker!"
He was dead, of course (on screen in the other room).

War seemed funny to him. My mom didn't understand,
yet she certainly didn't want to see it for the hundredth time,
unlike the romantic comedies she normally watched
every week, because she had nothing else to do, really.
I know it's just a movie
but the desensitization to such a horrid affair
as war and genocide, especially the pointless deathtrap
profit-power-grab-test-run, drug-trade-take-over,
that was Vietnam
angered me. A war 'lost,' yet our elite still won,
because the point was never to 'win,' but to profit.
At least no one in my immediate household was shooting up
some of the heroin smuggled into the country
by banking, military, and intelligence agencies,
stuffed into the corpses of dead U.S. soldiers.
I digress. It's more understandable in people like my parents
to not grasp this programming,
than others who should know better.
"Would you shut it off already?" my mom yelled.
"I want to watch TV!"   Television *programming*.
My mother has Cerebral Palsy. Lives in a wheelchair.
She was mostly ignored by her side of the family.
Mentality of a five-year-old. Virtually illiterate.
Talks to the pets in made-up baby-talk gibberish,
or yells demands at them as if they actually understand.
Hoarder of useless things. Innocent heart of a child.
Bitter scorn of one who has suffered.
Aware of her 'short-comings'—the hand she was dealt.
Sometimes, in certain situations, like when she wanted to help,
she'd say "I know I'm stupid…" and pout,
or sigh and say "I miss my mom…" when she was sad.
If you were around, she would go out of her way to say something,
anything, just to talk and break the silence,
to get your attention, even if it was about the same things

over and over:
the cats, the dog, that she's too cold or too hot, or tired,
something she saw on TV,
a picture in a magazine she could not read.
She'll make up any excuse to knock on my door,
like to ask me what time I went to work,
even if it's been the same time for months.
I feel terrible when I lose patience with her,
and when I have to remind myself that she or my father
simply will never understand many things.
They will never even be able to read this!
It breaks my heart and annoys me simultaneously,
to see her put herself down for what is out of her control,
and I hated myself sometimes
for not always wanting to entertain conversations with them.
I felt if anyone should be more tolerant, more respectful, it's me.
I felt insensitive, ashamed. But my knowledge separated me,
not always in a good way, because sometimes I could be cold.
And no matter how many times I cleaned the house,
it slowly turned back into a dump....
Their two children are their greatest accomplishments,
besides my mom learning English
when she came from Cuba for surgery (and never left),
and still surviving in this world (with help, of course).
Sometimes I felt guilty even for just going out,
especially in winter, because they stayed home most of the time,
and always for not making enough money
so we could all live more comfortably.
It's so strange lying in a room full of books,
opening up entire worlds to me,
and hearing such things outside my door
at 8 AM, from my mother and father, so utterly trapped
in themselves—unable to access these worlds.
Unable to read the signs in our environment

of approaching storms.
Sometimes I felt like I was born to read these signs,
to fulfill what they could not.
An unfortunate 'Millennial,'
early-bloomer in a multitude of ways, late bloomer in others,
constantly reminded that he already has children
who occasionally behave like adults,
before even being capable of taking care of himself.
I felt sorry for them, for myself,
for my brother, whom it was hard to blame for moving out,
and *him*, with his own set of burdens and his own family,
who it was also hard to blame for distancing himself
from dealing with my personality and these burdens.
But especially my grandmother, who raised us through it all;
first her own children and then my brother and I
for over 25 years, sacrificing her own dreams,
fulfilling the parental roles my parents could not,
taking care of them as well; giving me a sense of spirituality;
debating with me; learning with me; growing with me;
taking me out to eat and to the movies,
driving us everywhere, writing out the checks,
balancing the budget, paying the mortgage,
for our dingy century-old duplex on South Street.
She's the strongest person I know—my other mother,
the Matriarch, the Wise Woman full of life experience.
The survivor.
But even though I had her in mind,
and my friend was sleeping over, lying on blankets on my floor,
I still felt absolutely alone.
Like no one I desired would ever stay with me the way I wished,
with my baggage and theirs as one baggage.
I missed *him*…
I missed his voice, his embrace, his scent,
his silly laugh, his goofy jokes, his lips,

our bookish talks, even just watching him sleep;
the way he listened to me, all of my sorrowful repetitions,
political rants, spiritual meanderings, fringe research, sentiments,
fears of the future and intrigues of the past.
The way I held him; the way he held me when I cried,
when the weight of the world became too much to bear.
Do I really miss him or an idea I constructed of him?
Something I projected onto him? Did he *really* listen?
Just fight it! I think. *Stop feeling sorry for yourself!*
Is it really all just oxytocin, dopamine, and opiates?
I felt like a machine again, an addict
seeking the comfort of habit—I wanted control!
I felt it in my bones and wished he could feel it, too,
understand the same irritation I had with myself,
and the constant sense of urgency
to gather information—to keep learning for the sake of learning,
to keep a close eye out on the world, to record, read, write.
How trapped I felt in this house…
and that stench in the air of the whole country,
house of this house,
the stench Sebastian Haffner smelled in 1930's Germany:
the world entering another dangerous period, a pathocracy
with fancier gadgets! Mechanical war dogs and drones!
I could feel it. The inner essence of humanity the same,
the only difference being the toys were more efficient now.
Who knows what they could do?
Yet I *did* just finish reading Haffner's memoir
the night prior. Perhaps it was just residual paranoia?
Pertaining to the shootings in France, the psy-op,
the rampant censorship, civil war provocations,
spinning a manufactured 'clash of civilizations,'
the drums of war beating, battering ram upon my doorstep,
playing upon our fears, our religious beliefs, political extremism,
all of us pawns on a bankers' chessboard!

And then waking up to hear Full Metal Jacket on *again*,
listening to parental obliviousness, blissful ignorance.
Sometimes I thought they were luckier to not understand.
to not know, to talk to the cats and laugh, watch TV and eat.
Sometimes I wished I could unknow what I know.
Then I shake it off! I have to!
I wanted help, even a lover, yes, but no more expectations,
no more relying on others,
and no more taking knowledge for granted.
My knowing anything at all *is* my gift, my role in all of this.
Nevertheless, the fear of waking up
to find any remnant of an individual life,
my voice, my family, my friends,
snatched up from under me, like Haffner—
an economic collapse, or a great war to awaken!
Overt war, the war on our psyche already in place.
I read the signs, keeping an eye out.
To be put to sleep…
it gnawed at my mind like a parasite.
How could I possibly save my family
if shit ever *really* hit the fan here,
when I cannot even save myself yet?
What will the unfolding of the Cosmos bring us in death?
Sometimes I just want to escape, to run away,
shed my city conditioning and live in the mountains,
or a forest, sequestered; pull a Walden like Thoreau.
Right now, to *at least* just go back to sleep!
But the TV, *it's always on!*
"A day without blood is like a day without sunshine."
I bleed in the sunshine, in the open,
on a page for your eyes to collect and cage.

Programming a Generation (Delete Dissenters)

Turned 11 on the 9th day
of the 9th month.
Two days later, the 11th:
morning of demolition drama.
Sitting at a desk, near the window.
Ms. Lopez turns on the
tell-your-vision (what to see):
         Powerful images.
         A steel pillar burns
         on the screen.
         Another plane
         strikes the second.
         Returned home early
         that afternoon. *Red alert*
         —fear signals bombarding
            the bombarded.
         "America under attack!"
I was too young to
      understand. Now I see:
psychological assault
      on the populace
from within. 21st Century
      Reichstag burning?
      Crown of Capital,
      held aloft by the Pillars of Hercules. Sacrificed.

Historical rhyming, not repetition,
yet a stench I smelled as a child,
and began to trace as an adolescent.
The stench of—
                    cindered wires,
                    pulverized concrete,
                    mixed with bodies
        from my backyard
                    for over a week.
The stench of—

                    Indefinite war, manufactured
                        terror, FBI informants,
                    surveillance, Homeland Security,
                        'Patriot' Act, NDAA, TSA,
                            torture,
                        Guantanamo, Abu Ghraib,
                    increased militarism,
                        millions sacrificed,
                    occupation, resources siphoned,
                        black gold,
                    drones, drones, drones,
                        death from the sky,
                    Central Intel coups, proxy wars,
                        and drug smuggling,
                                'the other'-phobia,
                    Live in phobia! Ignorance is strength.
                        terror buzzwords,
                        media missiles,
                    fear the 'other'!—

                    lingers in my backyard
                                still....

        An environment transformed

66

under our noses. Before our eyes,
fed to us by a screen, a peddled narrative.
I am Post-9/11
generation, generated,
trying to deprogram

myself,
weaving through
droves of drones on ground,
complimenting the sky.
Kissing the sun, trying to be thankful for life,
to be grateful.
Music, art, friends, a struggling family, yet a family alive!
(Not bombed to smithereens)
Reading, drumming, smoking, sipping coffee, petting my cat,
some 'freedom' (privilege) to entertain myself,
eating poisoned food, the same as you,
from a grocery store.
An aching heart.
Restaurant drudgery and student loan debt.
No car, hardly any currency.
Filling a room with books
trying to catch up to reading them all.
Vocal on the internet. Loved and detested;
anathema for dissenting,
asking questions, trying to ameliorate.
A little odd, perhaps, but in a bundle of ways,
I am like you.

I am an
American.
Born and
raised
in a cage
with more
elbow room

　　　　　　　　　than most,
　　　　　　　　　　　yet
　　　　　　　　　shrinking—
　　　　　　　　　at the price
　　　　　　　　　of blood.

　　　Probably on a list for what I read,
　　　write, speak, and think,
　　　in my own country on the brink.

The nebulous 'they'

　　　keeping an eye out—
　　　rhyme historical,
　　　metaphorical.
　　　Now the gadgets are fancier. G. was right:
　　　'The outward form changes but the inner
　　　essence of man remains the same.'
　　　The intellectuals and savages. Machines.

　　　Watching, recording, storing,
from cellphones, satellites, street cameras, internet searches,
transactions, transportation, social media—
data-mine, data mine!
Data-mining
　　　　　　for mind-molding.
No, this isn't paranoia—this is reality. This is history.

Assessment, Manipulation, Abandonment.
　　　Control, Alter, Delete.
The task managers repeat;
　　　pathological preying party.
Assuaging our fears;
　　　　　'protection'
　　　　　　　supersedes

68

privacy and free speech,
until:

Ctrl   Alt

Delete

dissenters

Deep Roots

Dig your roots
deep,
    collect nourishment.
Spread your branches
        wide,
collect
    the Rays of Life.

The child who drowns
ants for entertainment
can still grow
    into and out-to
the man who watches
    where he's going,
who looks down
    as he strides, avoiding
every bug in sight
when he can.
        Yet understands
    not everyone is 'saved.' Must save ourselves,
    get out of the way if we can.
Searches
the ground
like a squirrel,
for acorns of
knowledge.

Saves himself.
Sometimes a savior.
Sometimes needs saving.
                    Searches the sky
                like a blue jay
                for debris to build
                his nest.
        Knows twigs made of Truth
        produce the strongest
foundation,
        They are stern
and will hold in times of need.
        That twigs hollowed
by deception
are brittle and snap
underneath your weight.

The child who drowns
ants just for fun
can still grow into
a man who drowns
other men,
made hollow by
emotional shallowness
inside
thinking he is full
of power,
because he can
snuff out forms.
                    Little does he know
                    that true power
                    preserves forms
and composes them
from previous forms

71

collected—it is *gnosis* collected.
Every twig and acorn
gathered
for the Soul's Winter.
Such a winter always
holds the potential
for Spring,
for non-being is
the illusion
and Being
the One true Infinite
Cosmic Potential.

Your roots are my branches,
my branches Your roots

Backyard

Prodigious product-placement place-mat,
product of the Market Revolution
and the Industrial Age, ostensibly auspicious.
Meta-metropolis, hub of American consumerism,
yet Horn of Amalthea filled
with beautiful cross-cultural collaboration,
synthesis, technology, prestidigitation.
Melting pot. Quagmires and quandary.
Trains, subway catacombs, an anthill with open guitar cases
and homeless musicians, those going to and from their 'jobs'
through tracks in underground mazes.
NJ-Transit, Penn Station, Grand Central, Port Authority.
Traversing Times Square, Union Square, Washington Square,
Broadway and the Village—Uptown, Downtown,
    from Brooklyn to the Bronx.
    Tenements and brownstones.
    Sneaking onto the ice-skating-ring afterhours

with my brother and friends as a teenager.
Pot-smoking on ice age rocks in Central Park years later.
Starbucks on every other corner, McDonalds, street Halal.
Souvenir shops, drug stores, coffee shops, whatever shops.
Webster Hall, St. Mark's and one-dollar pizza slices.
Williamsburg brimming with youth, street art, cafes.
*A*merican *t*oo much *me*-ism; ATM machines.
Fashion Avenue, and stores with pieces of clothing
worth more than my whole paycheck.
Traffic full of outdated combustion engines,
little mechanical blood cells with biology in them.

    Concerts abundant, museum time machines.
    Oligarchs and their avarice in concrete trees
    and watchtowers. Robber barons in an Empire State.
    Artifices in a hive, a nation *under*going
    the largest wealth-gap since the Roaring 20's.
    Innovative entrepreneurs and globalization.
    Outsourced labor. Systematic poverty and miseducation
or total lack thereof, and the Ivey Leagues.
Big loans if you're not from big bucks.
Those imprisoned in their suitcases full of numbers
on Wall Street, hobbling through the veins and arteries.
In the shadows, drug dealing, smuggling, pay-offs, Black budget,
SAP's, coups, proxy war plans, law halls, media mogul tentacles.
Game shows, talk-shows, and movie theaters.

    Billboards, bill boards, chessboards galore—
    buy more, buy more, buy more! Lights from floor
    to sky, skyscraping my senses. Fiscal vitreous honeycombs.
    Stop and frisk, better chances if you're lighter-skinned.
    Mace, rubber bullets, body armor, and tear gas.
    Misfit marches with poster boards and umbrellas.
    The vagabonds and the downtrodden.
A youth culture drenched in entertainment,
partying and dancing inside of their prison bars,

roller-skating with Molly, looking for escape;
the ones searching in fungi or quickie-spirituality-strips,
sitting in meditation circles, looking for escape;
short-cuts, glimpses of another reality, yet
on a silver platter—squandered; no mental labor.
　　　All of us swimming in a COINTELPRO pool—
　　　and the ones really fighting back! Information warriors,
　　　trying their best, doing what they can with where they are,
　　　with what they have, going beyond the get and grab.
　　　A batch of the most progressive intellects, scholars,
　　　muckrakers, artists, seekers groveling in the dark
　　　for the light, in scattered enclaves amongst it all,
struggling to make sense of it! The mind games!
What an ambivalent den of lions and hounds, with bouquets
of flowers burgeoning through the cracked pavement
to say 'We all lived, too, in this madness! We are poetry!'
And the busy bees gathering the pollen—
the poetry of living, any knowledge around them,
to churn it into that bitter-sweet honey of wisdom.
　　　Traps on every turn in the maze: the information war.
　　　Wedge issues, CNN, NBC, CBS, ABC, the whole alphabet
　　　Fox-trotting through my TV in Jersey, spinning the drama,
　　　setting limits to the debate argued about on the streets,
　　　the atrium and ventricles of a young nation. Mind games!
　　　I have always been both enamored and repulsed
　　　by this place as I tasted its fruits, a big apple
of bombarding sensory overload. Our Berlin?
It is not my home, but culturally I live on its outskirts.
It is my backyard. It is the real *capital* of the United States—
the heart of the empire. The epitome of 'urban' around here,
making Elizabeth almost appear 'suburban' to me.
Running around, lining up, day to day, week to week.
Year to year. It is *the* city.

Cold,
coevally
covetous century;
cretinous, cultured,
carnivorous, canny, clever.
Collectively crammed clatter,
creativity, consternation, commotion,
consumerism. Cross-cultural collaboration.
Colors coalescing.

So many people, so close together, yet so far
away from each other, looking down, staring at screens.
Some searching for light, looking up at the stars.
Traversing inside our bodily temporal railway cars
through the portals of an American heart of darkness.

The Zenne

An apparition before me in a dream passed,
like a whirling dervish, the song of a nightingale.
A vision, so fleeting, I wished I could make it last.
Such a dream could not stay; it followed its own path.

I just cannot stop thinking of you dancing that night,
in a golden cloth wrapped around your hips,
bare body moving to music, a luminous wave of light.
I wanted to embrace you there, press against your lips.

Twisting hands, separating and intertwining,
feet moving in circles, hips swaying on my silver lining.
I am caught; I am enraptured; I was grateful beyond words,
to witness this Word of God before me, His music heard.

Should I ever behold a sight as beautiful as this again,
such perfect splendor as this being, this moment, so free,
I would be truly blessed by the Almighty Friend,
for He danced you into my heart, gave me much to see.

As I lay, I could not explain why, how, or even when
my soul opened to a zenne who can never be obtained.
A beautiful dream dancing in the Court of the Friend,
so close to me in this moment, yet distance maintained.

You see and dance on your own; I see and dance on mine, too.
Yet still I wondered: if only we could dance together!
To brave highs and lows, calm and stormy weather;
I would try my best to keep the rhythm with you.

Dancing into my life. I into yours.
It's such a mystery to open another's door

A lonely poet dreamed.

Laughing at the Dinner Table

Life felt like a battle, a blow after blow.
Took an emotional one today, facing the hard truth:
too many barriers
kept people like us from being together.
Afterward he took me upstairs to eat with his parents.
His father invited me to sit down for dinner with them.
We were introduced. Shook hands, exchanged smiles.
As I walked through the house I tried to take everything in.
On the walls hung verses from the Qur'an.
Everything was tidy, the table was set.
I walked into the living room to look around before sitting.
Stared at all of the family photos in frames,
on the walls, on surfaces—mostly of two sisters and a brother.
I told them how beautiful their home was. I meant it.
Soon we sat down and passed around the portions.
Delicious salmon in olive oil with lemon and pepper,
a bowl of pasta, glasses of water,
salad with black olives and chopped tomatoes.
I asked about the salmon recipe so I could make it at home.
His mother and father had the most welcoming demeanor,
their hospitality abundant, manners respectful.
She wore a light pink hijab, her smile radiant, voice pleasant.
He was funny, kind, with a thick gray mustache, hearty laugh.
They truly were wonderful people.
They were 'normal' parents, the opposite of my own…
I looked at all of the stuff on the refrigerator as I ate:
a bunch of souvenir Elizabeth Tower magnets from London,
pictures of grandparents, uncles, aunts, cousins.

They joked about another friend of his,
how they once offered him salad:
"Have more salad! Americans love salad!" they said, chuckling.
I found the joke heartwarming, because when I looked at them
I also saw Americans.
I didn't feel any more 'American' than them.
Sure, they carried their traditions closer, which I envied
(individualism consumed my family's long ago,
through generations)
but they were still Americans.
Their traditions and culture just another contribution
to the conversation: the culture of our nation.
Eventually they asked how I met their son.
The internet, a mutual friend.
I picked up on the slight tension behind his answers.
We left it at that.
Talked a bit about where I lived and went to school.
He mentioned the Palestine protest I attended.
I briefly expressed my outrage; we cracked some more jokes,
obviously to lighten the mood of this dark topic.
Once the conversation shifted slightly into politics
I could feel a change.
They made a joke that I might be on a list for protesting,
especially now that I was sitting there eating dinner with *them*.
We all laughed, but I felt horrible inside.
This is really happening…
They even joked about being on a watch-list themselves.
Stories were told of getting pulled out of lines at airports
because of their names, or the way they looked;
and of always getting suspicious stares from people.
My heart continued to sink. I kept smiling, but I was crying inside,
partly for selfish reasons, partly for selfless ones.
First, being unable to ever be a part of this kind of family
bothered me;

81

not only being unable to ever marry into one,
but simply not having one of my own like this,
to have someone else marry into it.
I wasn't exactly sure why I envied it, or why I wished I had it.
I suppose it was because of how run-down my home felt
in comparison, how vastly different my family was.
And how ungrateful I felt for thinking such thoughts.
I guess I wished I had some kind of heritage like this,
that my family at least ate together when everyone was around.
My grandmother said she always tried to get us to,
but we were too sucked up in television,
video games, friends, and so on, eating alone in our rooms.
The barriers between he and I
stabbed at my heart like a twisting knife;
after eating with them I could see why he would not risk losing this
by being with someone like me.
I had none of this to give anyone or even to risk losing.
Despite hiding a part of himself from some family members,
I saw why he valued traditions more.
And to be alone was his choice, as much as it burned me.
Second, on top of envy,
I felt powerless to lift the oppressive air over them.
We laughed at these political things, but I could feel the tension,
the absolute seriousness behind our laughing.
I had a knot in my stomach, a sinking feeling behind my smile.
The whole experience
made me think of Haffner's book again,
how scared he was for his Jewish girlfriend,
how her family also joked amongst each other about it,
to take the edge off,
as they knew Germany was changing and turning against them.
These wonderful, humble people were worried.
They felt unsafe in their own home.
Well aware of the conflicts outside this roof, the changes.

Well aware that they were targeted and watched
by their own government, as American citizens.
These weren't 'terrorists,' these weren't 'outsiders.'
They weren't 'others.' Our sisters and brothers!
There was no agenda here at all.
I kept thinking:
if I went into any average suburban American home,
replaced the photos there with his family's,
replaced all of the crucifixes
with plaques of verses from the Qur'an,
I would hardly feel or notice a difference here at all.
Such good, kind people. I was grateful to dine with them.
I felt comfortable around them,
despite how I suspected they might feel
if they knew about my sexuality,
my own manner-less tradition-less family
and what they were really like,
or all my maverick views on spirituality.
Yet I still felt welcome there.
I felt I could somehow relate to them, even if I could not be candid.
Perhaps because the prejudice that hurts them, in essence,
is the same as the prejudice
which hurts me because of my sexuality.
If only we could go beyond all prejudices and beliefs,
grow and transform them,
still holding onto our individualism,
yet maintain that essence of unity,
the etymological root of religion—of tradition, of culture. To bind!
If only we could reconcile our barriers,
the invisible boarders. To bind!
Our careers, beliefs, fears, and families. To bind!
The fearful walls we erect between our hearts and minds.
Maybe then we could fall in love…
But it was just a fantasy in my head. One I knew could never be.

This world was such a frightening, lonely place sometimes—
a jungle, a dinner table we all laughed at to take the edge off.
Perhaps I was just paranoid,
but I feared for their lives more than my own.
I feared for him.

Spoken by God (We Fit) in the Goddess

Mount Meru
The World Tree
undulation
around a Sacred Axis
circumvolution
Mandala of Mouths
spiraling around
Centre of Centers
radial
<O>
'BELOW'
subatomic
atomic
molecular
cellular
bacterial
insecta
animalia
humanoid
human
'alien'
Beyond
'ABOVE'

<O>
circumfluent
of and within
(Womb) Mind
of
(Goddess) God
we are spoken
our lives uttered
inhaled
exhaled
solve et coagula
within an athanor
figure eight
even
odd
like atoms
it's how we're shaped
how we fit together
dense
or loose
charged
positive
negative
everything in-between
neutrons
neurons
star dust
carbon atoms
side by side
one moment
knocking out
restoring
each other's protons
created like plutonium

destroying like it
each moment
a spectrum
circumspection
floating around
various states of matter
genetic codes
fitting where we fit
electrons we lack
add or subtract
divide and multiply
we transform
bonds made
bonds broken
we are enzymes
catalysts
neurotransmitters
receptors
waves
electrical pulses
molecules that fit
where we fit
like keys
like words

an urban Argonaut
cantillating in cant

Old Friends

Birds leap from bough to branch,
building nests, growing wings,
taking flight within a cattle ranch.
Dipteral, hearts and minds sing.

Soaking in symbols with the eye,
a thousand lives lived to bloom.
Immortally staining a page to fly
through the window of your room.

Converse between ages, old friends
forever speaking to *you* directly.
We are a story which never ends,
a story spoken spectrally

ABOUT THE AUTHOR

Daniel DeLafe was born and raised in Elizabeth, New Jersey, where he still resides. In 2014 he received his B.A. in English & Writing from Kean University. He is an independent bookseller, a book collector, and an avid reader with an epic curiosity, fascinated by everything from history, comparative religion, mythology, psychology, the paranormal, esotericism and the occult, to science, world literature, poetry, and art. He occasionally enjoys drawing and painting, is a self-taught drummer/percussionist, and is partial to the company of cats, although he loves dogs as well. This is his first book of poetry.

"Ora, Lege, Lege, Lege, Relege, Labora et Invenies."

— *Mutus Liber*, plate 14

Made in the USA
Monee, IL
25 January 2022

89892812R00062